The Day My Brain Went CRAZY

Michelle Karavas

creative
PUBLISHING

Published in Australia by Creative Publishing
Postal: PO Box 910 Macleod West Vic 3085
Email: michellekaravas@gmail.com
Website: www.michellekaravas.com.au

First published in Australia 2017

A catalogue record for this book is available from the National Library of Australia

National Library of Australia Cataloguing-in-Publication entry

Creator: Karavas, Michelle, author.

Title: The day my brain went crazy / Michelle Karavas.

ISBN: 978-0-99-455560-1 (Hardback)
ISBN: 978-0-9945556-3-2 (Createspace paperback)
ISBN: 978-0-99-455561-8 (eBook PDF)
ISBN: 978-0-9945556-4-9 (mobi)

Target Audience: For primary school age.

Subjects: Anger in children - Juvenile fiction.
Temper - Juvenile fiction.
Children's stories.

Other Creators / Contributors: Gottardo, Angela, illustrator.

Printed by Createspace

Dedication

To my son Aidan:

You have been the inspiration for this book. Without your help, it would

not have been created. Although you have a fiery temperament at

times, you are a beautiful, spirited little boy.

To my son Caleb:

Thank you for being there to support me with this book. You have been

a great help, allowing me to bounce ideas off you whenever I needed.

You boys are my world, and I love you very much.

Does your brain ever go crazy? Have you ever felt like you can't control your feelings or behaviour? That you think you're going to explode? Jake has, and he calls it: 'The day my brain went crazy!'

Jake is 8 years old. He has bright blue eyes and curly blonde hair. He lives with his mum and dad, older brother Robbie, and their dog Milo.

Jake is very good at sports like basketball, and he loves to draw and play video games. He's a funny kid who makes people laugh, and he's happy most of the time. Sometimes though, Jake gets angry. He's good at controlling his anger in public, but when he gets home he lets it all out!

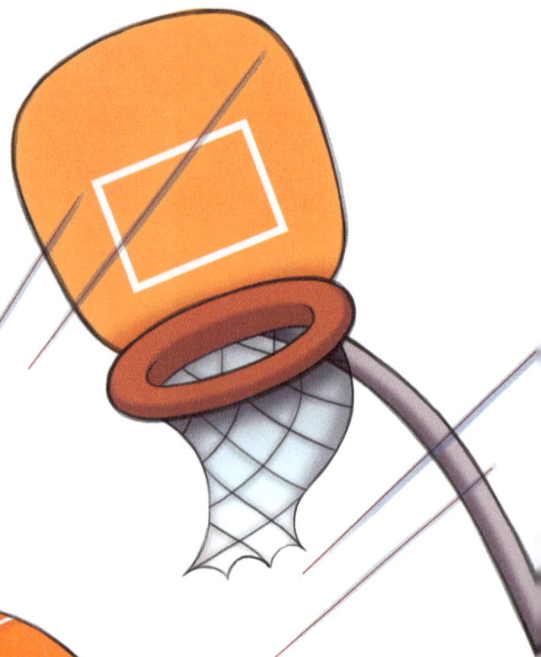

There are SO many things that make Jake angry. If Jake spells a word wrong on his homework, that makes him angry. When Jake plays games on his Xbox® and gets attacked by a zombie, guess what? He gets angry. Sometimes his brother Robbie teases Jake about being better at basketball, and this makes him angry too.

One Saturday morning, Jake woke in his cosy bed, all snuggled up in his favourite blanket. He smiled as he remembered his dream about playing basketball with his friends. He felt calm and happy.

After eating his breakfast, Jake's dad asked him to help with some jobs around the house.

"Jake, can you please clean your room, put your shoes away, and pack up your toys?" his dad asked.

All of a sudden Jake's head felt like it was going to explode. He thought he could feel steam coming out of his ears. He was ANGRY!

That is when 'IT' happened. Jake's brain started to go crazy. His face turned red. His heart started thumping, and he clenched his hands.

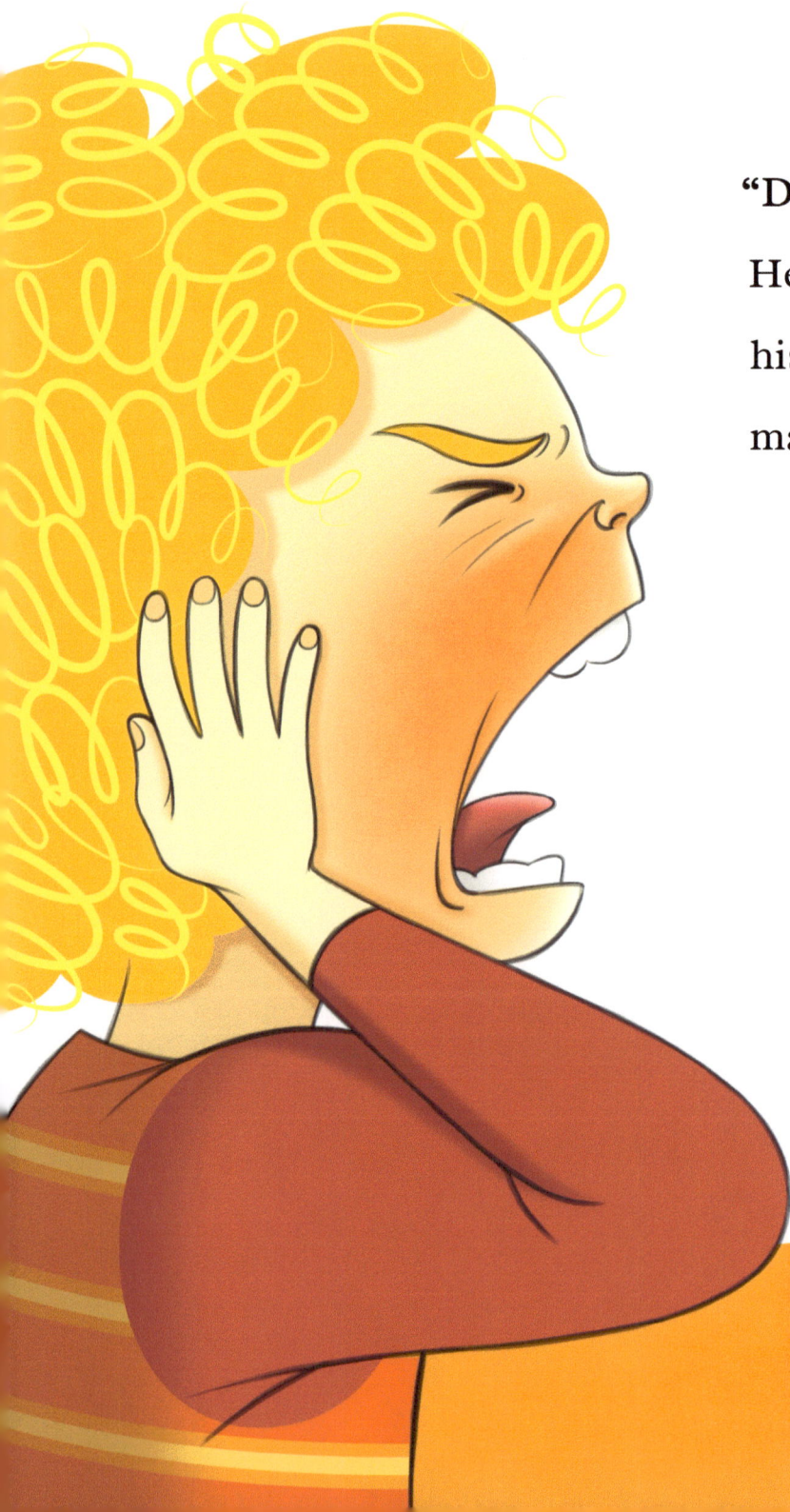

"Dad, STOP!" Jake yelled.

He covered his ears because

his dad was giving him too

many instructions all at once.

Jake took off, running around the house screaming as loud as his voice would go. He ran to his bedroom and slammed the door so hard the picture frame on his mum's cabinet fell to the floor.

Jake started to wreck his room. He pulled his posters from the wall, threw his toys around, and stomped his feet on the floor, screaming the whole time.

After he finished screaming, Jake was exhausted. He sat on the floor with tears streaming from his eyes. Jake whispered to himself, *"Why is my brain going crazy?"*

You see, when Jake's brain goes crazy he feels like he can't understand instructions. The anger gets trapped in his head, and he doesn't know how to calm down. Jake needs help.

Jake's mum came into his room. She slowly and carefully gave him a big hug. She also started to rub Jake's back, as she knew that was one of his favourite things.

"I'm sorry, Mum," said Jake. "I'm sorry for getting angry."

His mum looked at him and said, "Your brain really went crazy this time, Jake."

"Yeah, I know," he said. "I should have remembered to look at my Calm Chart."

The last time Jake had lost his temper, his mum helped him make a chart to hang on his bedroom door. It gave Jake ideas about how to calm down when he felt angry. It said:

Jake's Calm Chart

When I feel angry I can:

1 - Punch a pillow or mattress

2 - Jump on the trampoline

3 - Scream into a pillow

4 - Go outside and kick a ball

5 - Scribble on a piece of paper,

then scrunch it up and throw it away

6 - Squeeze lemons

(when you pretend you have

lemons in your hands and you

squeeze them so hard, they burst!)

"It's okay," said Jake's mum. "Next time you feel angry, will you try to remember to look at the chart?"

"I'll try," Jake agreed.

The next day, Jake sat eating dinner with his family. He was feeling frustrated with his mum and dad because they asked him to eat ALL his vegetables. He wasn't allowed to leave the table until he did. But Jake hates vegetables, especially broccoli! Jake also doesn't like being told what to do, or hearing the word 'NO'.

All of a sudden, Jake had that feeling again. Was his brain about to go crazy? He could feel his face turning red and his teeth grinding together. When his heart started to thump wildly, he knew what to do. He remembered.

Jake raced off to his bedroom
and quickly looked at his
Calm Chart. He chose two
things: he screamed into his
pillow, and then punched his
mattress. After a few minutes,
Jake's anger began to go down,
and he felt much calmer.

Jake walked quietly back to the dinner table and sat down calmly. His parents could see how exhausted he was from all the screaming and punching. Jake began to eat his vegetables, just like his mum and dad had asked him.

"Well done, Jake," said his mum. "I'm proud of you for remembering to use your Calm Chart. I can see how it helped you to feel better."

Jake didn't say much but felt a small grin creep onto his face. He knew he had made the right choice.

"Jake, you did a really great thing tonight by calming down on your own. Why don't we all watch a movie to celebrate? Your pick," said his mum with a smile.

Now Jake felt the opposite of anger. He felt happy! He had wanted to watch *The LEGO® Movie* for ages. He was so excited to be rewarded for managing his anger in a calm way.

Jake, Mum, Dad, and Robbie got some popcorn ready. They all snuggled onto the couch and watched the *LEGO*® characters come on screen.

Jake's brain felt less crazy. His family was proud of him, but most importantly, he was proud of himself. Smiling, he thought *"This is the best night ever"*.

About the Author

Michelle Karavas is a child psychologist and has worked for the Department of Education and Training in both primary and secondary school settings for thirteen years. She counsels children and adolescents who have difficulties with anxiety, depression, grief, stress, autism, social skills, anger, and bullying.

Along with her private practice, Michelle has worked with young offenders in the Juvenile Justice System and has run a number of group programs for young people.

She was inspired to write this book after working with many children – including her own – to help them better manage their emotions. Michelle hopes this book will help children learn a variety of ways to manage their feelings, particularly when they are angry. She also hopes this book gives parents an opportunity to open a dialogue with their children about their emotions.

Michelle lives in Melbourne with her husband and two sons.

Notes for Parents

What is anger?

Anger is a completely normal human emotion. Often it is in reaction to frustration, stress, disappointment, or even when children don't get their own way. It's okay to feel angry at times, and it is actually important to get angry at times.

Who feels angry?

We all feel angry sometime or another. As children grow, most learn how to deal with the frustrations of everyday life, and they learn helpful ways to manage their anger. However, some children need a little more help when it comes to managing their emotions in healthy ways.

Is this normal?

We all experience a range of emotions. Sometimes we may feel happy, sad, jealous, or scared. Anger is just another emotion we feel, and it is completely normal to feel angry.

However, some children find it tricky to manage their anger and have difficulty regulating their emotions. Some children can go from 0 to 100 without warning.

Others are like a volcano that is about to explode!

What to do?

It is important to teach children that all feelings are healthy and normal; however, children often need tools to learn how to best manage their emotions. Using an emotional vocabulary with children is important as it normalises it for them, and shows the child that you accept and validate their feelings.

Children need the assistance of adults to help them learn to use words rather than aggressive actions to communicate their feelings. If they don't have the proper emotional tools, that is when anger can get out of control and children can start to hurt others, themselves, or damage property.

As children understand and communicate at different levels, visuals (or pictures) can also be used to help a child communicate. It is a great tool to help them see and understand what they are being asked to do, especially when they are in a highly emotional state. When a child is in this state they can feel overwhelmed when too much language is being spoken to them, and they can then feel too overwhelmed to also read instructions. This can then make a child angrier.

Visuals give the child the ability to process the information in their own time. They act as a cue to inform children what they can do and simplify the message by breaking it down into small, achievable steps.

Visual supports can be used to help children learn ways in which they can better communicate with others and for parents or teachers to communicate effectively with the child.

Parents, caregivers, and school staff play an important role in helping children learn to manage anger effectively. They can begin by teaching children to look for the warning signs in their body when they start to feel angry. For example, children will say their heart is beating fast, their face is turning red, and their hands are clenching.

Some children keep their anger bottled up inside, causing them to get a headache, sore stomach, or just feel sad and cry.

Our body is our best friend. It gives us warning signs to let us know that we are feeling a particular way. As adults we can help children tune into these warning signs so they can better self-regulate.

As adults and educators, it is important for us to be aware that it is not always easy for children to know or verbalise what is bothering them. Therefore, they may not want to talk about it. It is important as parents, family members, and educators to model how we effectively manage our own feelings. By acting calmly, we can help reassure children that they are capable of successfully managing their own difficult feelings.

Everyone has feelings. It takes time and patience to learn how to manage them effectively.

www.ingramcontent.com/pod-product-compliance
Lightning Source LLC
Chambersburg PA
CBHW061059090426
42742CB00003B/100